D0842772

 for the Hostess

Better Homes & Gardens

JUNIOR Cook Book

and Host of tomorrow

Meredith Press, Des Moines

Revised Edition. Third Printing
© Meredith Publishing Company, 1963. All rights reserved
Copyright Meredith Publishing Company 1955. All rights reserved
Printed in the United States of America

Cooking can

be so easy

*It's fun to learn to make sizzly hamburgers, thick chocolate
shakes, beautiful gooey rolls—all of the delicious foods
you love to eat. Cook your favorites the simple and safe way.*

Talk it over with Cook, Sr.

Ask your mother to tell you how to use
the range. Or maybe you already know?
She'll think it's really wonderful to have a
Junior Cook—you can count on her for
help. Talk over your recipe with her, make
sure that you are not out of some of the
ingredients before starting to cook.

About drips

Wipe your hands very dry after you wash
them. Wet hands are slippery—regular
"butter fingers." Wipe up spills on the
floor right away so someone doesn't slip
and fall. And now have a look at you—
you're spotlessly clean of course, and
your hair's neat and brushed back. How
about wearing a spanking-clean apron?

Watch out for ouches!

Sure as a pot's hot, you'll say *ouch* if you
don't use a potholder. Steady handle with
a holder while you stir. When you take
hot dishes out of the oven, use a holder in
each hand. Pull the oven rack out a little
way to make the job easier. Set hot pans
on a cooling rack, hot pad, or on counter
top the heat doesn't hurt.

Pare off this way

Cut away from yourself when you use a
vegetable parer. Hold the vegetable in
one hand, the parer in the other. Watch
out for the fingers. If you're slicing or
dicing, do the job on a wood chopping
board so you won't damage the counter.
Always check to see that "all's clear."

Cool hand, hot pot

Stir hot mixture with a wooden spoon or
a metal spoon with a wood or a plastic
handle. An all-metal spoon gets hot; hot
enough to burn. If you leave the range
for just a minute, turn handle of pan so
no one will bump the pan and spill it. Also,
use the wooden spoon for beating; it plays
the part of your silent helper.

How to put in a plug

Be sure your hands are dry when you plug
in or disconnect an appliance. When you
are through using the appliance, take hold
of the plug and pull straight out. Don't
pull on the cord—you may loosen the
wires inside the plug. Remember—always
unplug the appliance cord from wall *first*
—then take cord from appliance.

←*Saucy Franks, page 50, give you plenty of spicy sauce for the buns*

Wise up to cooking terms

Stir—To mix around and around with a spoon or fork. Usually you use a spoon, but use a fork to stir pastry.

Whip—Use egg beater to whip rich cream or beat egg whites till light and fluffy. This "whipping" adds air.

Chop—This means to cut in pieces with knife, scissors, or chopper. Here, celery is being chopped on wood.

Bake—Cook in the oven. You bake cookies, cakes, and many casseroles.

Baste—Pour liquid over food while it cooks. You baste some meats in the oven.

Beat—Mix *fast* with beater or a spoon. Beating takes a little muscle or your mother's electric beater. If beating by hand, lift mixture with each beat.

Blend—Mix the ingredients until they are smooth.

Boil—Cook until liquid is so hot it bubbles hard and steams.

Broil—Cook by direct heat. You can use broiler. Or, broil over coals at barbecues.

Brush—Spread thinly with a brush. Or, maybe clean fingers will do the job.

Combine—Mix ingredients.

Cream—To beat shortening until it is creamy and fluffy. Or, cream sugar *and* shortening.

Dice—To cut food into small cubes of same size and shape.

Fold—Mix ingredients with a rubber spatula, whisk, or spoon. This is a special, gentle way of mixing. To fold, cut down through the mixture, across bottom of bowl, up and over top, close to surface of mixture. Fold like this over and over.

Fry—Cook in hot fat.

Garnish—Make food look as good as it tastes. A bright-red cherry can garnish an ice-cream sundae. A sprig of mint garnishes a cool, lime beverage.

Melt—Make liquid by heating.

Mix—Stir ingredients together.

Pare—Cut away the outside covering of fruits and vegetables. You *pare* a potato.

Peel—Strip off the outer covering. You *peel* a banana.

Pit—Take out the seeds.

Scald—Heat milk to just below boiling point. You'll see tiny bubbles just around the edge.

Sift—Put dry ingredients, like flour and baking powder, through sieve or sifter.

Simmer—Cook in liquid over very low heat.

Toss—Mix ingredients lightly. You toss salad greens.

How to measure up to good cooks

Successful cooking depends on correct measuring. It pays to be accurate. Always use special measuring cups and spoons—not the kind you use when you eat.

Liquids

Glass measuring cup has 1-cup mark below rim so you won't spill. Cup has a lip like a pitcher. Place cup on counter to measure liquids. Bend down and watch as you pour.

Shortening

Pick cup or spoon that holds amount the recipe calls for. Pack shortening so there won't be any air left in cup or spoon. Level off top with straight edge of a knife.

Dry ingredients

Pick cup or spoon that holds amount recipe calls for. Fill to overflowing. Level with knife. Careful—don't pack ingredients.

Brown sugar

Pick the right-size cup. Fill with brown sugar. Push down hard with spoon. Add more, pack down. Level off top with knife.

Chapter 1

Beverages

Frosty orange float

You'll need:

Orange sherbet   Chilled orange pop   Mint   Peppermint sticks

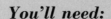

Take out: tall glasses, spoon, bottle opener

1 Mix a spoonful of sherbet and chilled pop in glass.

2 Fill it with orange pop. Float sherbet on the top.

3 Trim each with a sprig of mint, a peppermint stick.

Grape float

You'll need:	Chilled grape juice 	Chilled ginger ale	Orange sherbet
Take out:	glasses, spoons, bottle opener		

1 Take a glass the size you want. Fill half-full of grape juice. Use the bottled or frozen grape juice.

2 Next, slowly pour in the chilled ginger ale. Leave plenty of room in glass for the orange sherbet.

3 The sherbet goes in last. A big scoop looks nice. Easy does it! Not too big or it'll run over.

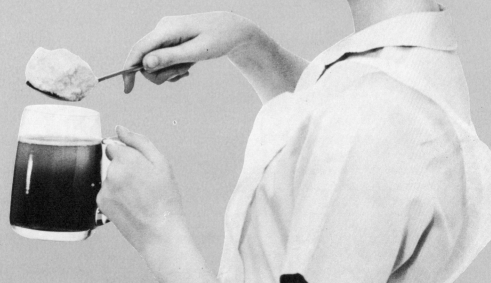

Simple-to-fix creamy COCOA

Take out:	saucepan, measuring spoons and cups, spoon, potholder, cups, saucers, ladle

You'll need:

5 tablespoons cocoa   Dash salt   5 tablespoons sugar

½ cup water   3½ cups milk   Marshmallows

Cook 3 minutes

1   Mix cocoa, salt, sugar, water in pan. Cook, and stir.

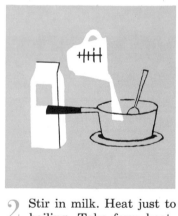

2   Stir in milk. Heat just to boiling. Take from heat.

3   Ladle into six cups. Add marshmallow tops, serve.

Rich chocolate

SHAKE

Take out:	covered jar or shaker, spoon, measuring spoons and cup, glass or mug
You'll need:	

| Vanilla ice cream | 2 tablespoons chocolate syrup | ½ cup milk |

1 Put about 5 big spoonfuls of ice cream in a shaker.

2 Add chocolate syrup. Mix a bit with spoon. Add milk.

3 Cover jar and shake hard. This makes one milk shake.

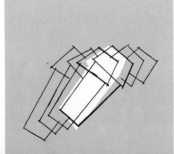

Use more ice cream to make the milk shake extra thick, rich.

Lime FIZZ

Take out:

paring knife
measuring cups
pitcher
spoon
glasses
bottle opener

You'll need:

½ cup lime juice

¾ cup
sugar

2 cups
water

2 7-ounce
bottles
carbonated
water

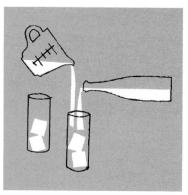

1 Measure lime juice. Put in a pitcher. Add sugar, water; stir. Add ice to the glasses.

2 Put about ½ cup lime mixture in glass. Fill with carbonated water. Add mint sprigs.

Tutti-frutti

Take out:

large pitcher or bowl
measuring cups
spoon   ice-cube trays
glasses
bottle opener

You'll need:

1 1-ounce package
each: orange, lime,
cherry summer-
drink powder

Sugar

Water

Chilled
lemon-lime
carbonated
beverage

1 Mix *each* flavor summer-drink powder with ⅔ cup sugar, 4 cups of water. Pour into separate cube trays; freeze.

2 To serve, put one cube of each of three flavors in big glass. Fill glass with lemon-lime carbonated beverage, chilled.

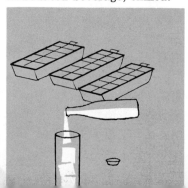

Eggnog

Take out:	You'll need:
mixing bowl	1 egg
egg beater	2 tablespoons
measuring	sugar
spoons	Dash salt
and cup	1 cup milk
glass and	½ teaspoon
straws	vanilla

1 Break egg into mixing bowl and beat with an egg beater until egg looks smooth, thick.

2 Add sugar and salt to egg. Then, beat until you can see that sugar, salt are dissolved.

3 Beat in milk and vanilla. Serve eggnog immediately. Makes one serving.

ce SPARKLE

Tall, tingling sparklers with colorful cubes—you'd better be ready with lots of refills.

CIRCUS TIME

lemonade

Just right for partytime or any time—lemonade and cookies. Be sure to try the quick-trick decoration for lemonade—tuck a sprig of mint in each glass. Or, slice a lemon and use it for trim.

Take out:	can opener, pitcher, spoon, glasses			
You'll need:	1 can frozen lemonade concentrate	Cold water	Ice cubes	Mint

1 Open a can of frozen lemonade concentrate. Empty the concentrate into a tall pitcher.

2 Add as much water as it says on side of the can and stir with spoon till well mixed.

3 Put ice cubes in glasses. Fill with lemonade. Add a mint sprig to top of each glass.

Ideas for

making extra-special beverages and good treats to serve with them

Fancy ice-cube coolers put plain pop in the special party class. To make these fancy coolers, freeze a red or green cherry in each of the ice cubes in an ice-cube tray. Or, try a pineapple chunk, a lime slice, or a perfect strawberry. First, wait until the ice has started to form around the sides and bottoms of the cubes and then add the fruit of your choice. This keeps the fruit centered in the cubes. Use the ice-cube coolers in glasses when you serve pop.

Pink Lemonade is easy. Just color the Circus Time Lemonade (page 16) with a few drops of red food coloring. The use of pink ice cubes makes this lemonade even prettier. To make pink ice cubes, freeze two 12-ounce bottles of strawberry pop in an ice-cube tray of refrigerator. This makes enough cubes to chill two recipes of Circus Time Lemonade.

Peppermint-stick stirrers to whirl in each mug of Cocoa (page 12) you serve add a surprise minty flavor. Serve the stirrers in cocoa to your friends after an ice-skating party.

Crispy popcorn is good by itself. You can make it taste even better by sprinkling a handful of salted nuts over a big bowlful of popcorn. Or you can sprinkle with Parmesan cheese for a snappy flavor that goes well with glasses of cider.

To make fluffy, hot popcorn: Pour 3 tablespoons of salad oil in a heavy saucepan that has a lid. Heat until a drop of water sizzles in the oil. Then, add ½ cup of popcorn. Put the lid on the pan. Shake pan over heat until the kernels have quit popping. Pour out fluffy snowflakes of popcorn into a bowl. Pour melted butter over it if you wish. Stir.

Quick, warm nibblers: Spread out tiny shredded-wheat wafers on a flat, cooky sheet. Sprinkle the wafers with seasoned salt and heat them until toasty in a 350° oven.

Cheese Chips are delicious to munch with chilled tomato juice or with Lime Fizz (page 14). To fix these crisp, hot chips, arrange potato chips on an ungreased cooky sheet. Sprinkle them with grated cheese and onion salt. Broil them in broiler until the cheese starts to bubble. Serve at once while chips are hot.

Doll-size sandwiches are quick and fun to make. Invite your guests to munch on nut halves that are sandwiched with dabs of a smoky cheese. Use California walnuts or pecans.

Shoestring potatoes from a can are crunchy and good to eat with beverages. Serve them with Grape Floats (page 11). Or, you can serve them with your favorite kind of pop.

Hot Spiced Pineapple-grapefruit Juice is perfect for wintertime parties. You can buy the combination juice in cans. Measure juice carefully as you put it in saucepan. For each cup of juice, add 2 whole cloves and a 1-inch stick of cinnamon. Then, simmer it over *very low* heat for about 5 minutes or until the juice is completely warm. Ladle into cups or mugs and serve with whole cinnamon-stick "stirrers." Take to your guests while juice is still warm. Everyone hungry? Pass a big plate of sugary doughnuts, or serve spicy, cinnamon doughnuts.

Chapter 2

Breads and Sandwiches

GOOEY ROLLS

You'll need:	Take out:
2 tablespoons honey	small bowl
2 tablespoons sugar	spoon
2 tablespoons soft butter or margarine	baking sheet
2 tablespoons flour	measuring spoons and cup
1 package brown-and-serve rolls	table knife
Nut halves	potholder

1 Set oven at 375°. Put honey, sugar, butter, and the flour in a small bowl. Mix the ingredients till well blended.

2 Put rolls on a baking sheet. Spread honey mixture on top of rolls. Then, arrange nut halves on top of each roll.

Bake about 15 minutes

3 Place baking sheet in the oven. Bake about 15 minutes. Serve rolls when hot. Don't worry about leftovers.

Biscuits

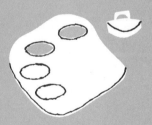

1 Set oven at 450°. Put biscuit mix in bowl; add milk. Stir vigorously with a fork until dough follows the fork around the bowl.

2 Dust rolling pin, pastry cloth with biscuit mix. Put dough on cloth; knead eight times. Roll out till dough's ½-inch thick.

3 Dip biscuit cutter in mix before cutting. Repeat each time. Place biscuits on ungreased sheet.

Bake about 12 minutes

4 Put in oven. Bake 10 to 15 minutes. Tops will be golden brown. The recipe makes about twelve biscuits.

You'll need:

2 cups biscuit mix   ⅔ cup milk

Take out:

mixing bowl and fork
measuring cups
pastry cloth or board
rolling pin
cooky sheet
turner
potholder
biscuit cutter

Flaky golden biscuits deserve to be whisked straight from the oven to table. They're delicious as bread, or drench them with syrup, butter.

Cherry fill-ups

Cherry-filled biscuits are early-bird fare. You can delight the family by fixing a treat for breakfast. Let Mother give you some help with other breakfast foods that go with these.

425°

1 Set the oven at 425°. Ask Mother to open the biscuits for you. Arrange biscuits in a round pan so they nearly touch.

You'll need:	cherry preserves, 1 package refrigerated biscuits, 2 tablespoons sugar, 1 egg, 2 tablespoons milk
Take out:	9-inch round pan, egg beater, measuring spoons, teaspoon, pastry brush, potholder, bowl, turner

2 Press tiny hollow in the center of each biscuit with your fingers. Fill hollow with a teaspoon of the preserves.

3 Break egg into a bowl and beat smooth with egg beater. Beat in sugar, milk. This glaze puts a shine on biscuits.

4 Brush on egg mixture with a pastry brush and then bake about 10 minutes. Remove them from pan. Serve at once.

Jelly muffins

You'll need:

⅓ cup shortening
1¾ cups sifted
   all-purpose flour
¾ cup milk
2½ teaspoons
   baking powder
1 egg
2 tablespoons
   sugar
¾ teaspoon salt
Jelly

Take out:

muffin pan
flour sifter
waxed paper
measuring cups
   and spoons
rubber scraper
bowls
egg beater
small skillet
spoons
potholder

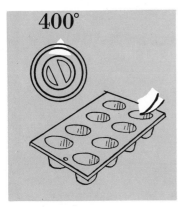

1 Set the oven at 400°. Then, lightly grease the muffin cups with a bit of fat. Or, use the little paper baking cups.

2 Measure the sifted flour, put in a small bowl. Add baking powder, sugar, and salt. Sift these into a larger bowl.

3 Put shortening in a small skillet and heat until it is melted. Remove skillet from the heat. Let it cool slightly.

4 Break the egg into a small bowl. Beat with egg beater until it's smooth. Add milk. Then, add melted shortening.

5 Make a hollow in center of flour mixture. Add the milk mixture. Stir *only* until dry ingredients have been moistened.

6 Fill the cups half full. Add teaspoon of jelly to each. Just cover the jelly with batter. Bake muffins about 25 minutes.

22

Butter-toasted sweet rolls

You'll need:

Sweet rolls   Soft butter or margarine

Take out:

bread knife   skillet   table knife
breadboard   turner   potholder

1 Slice sweet rolls in half. Spread them with soft butter or margarine.

2 Place butter-side-down in skillet. Toast over low heat till golden brown.

Cinnamon toast

You'll need:

1 slice bread   1 teaspoon sugar

Soft butter or margarine   ¼ teaspoon cinnamon

Take out:

toaster,   table knife,   measuring spoons

1 Toast bread in the toaster. Spread at once with butter.

2 Dust with sugar, cinnamon. Or mix ¼ cup sugar, 1 table-spoon cinnamon; use shaker.

Perfect French toast

You'll need:

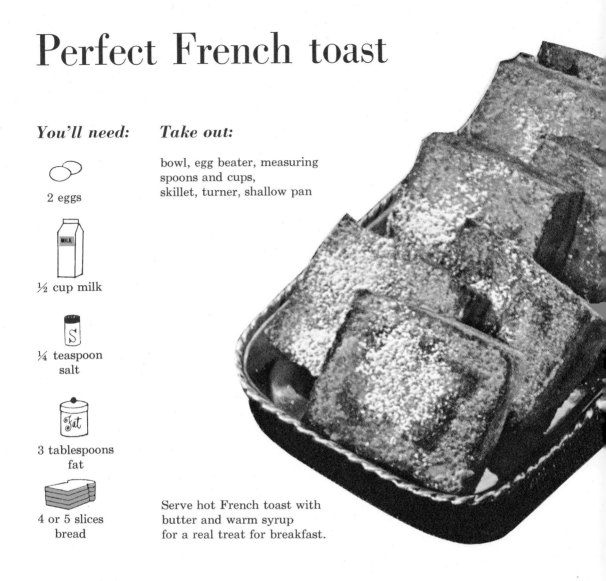

2 eggs

½ cup milk

¼ teaspoon
salt

3 tablespoons
fat

4 or 5 slices
bread

Take out:

bowl, egg beater, measuring
spoons and cups,
skillet, turner, shallow pan

Serve hot French toast with
butter and warm syrup
for a real treat for breakfast.

1 Break the eggs into a
bowl. Use egg beater and
beat until smooth, blended.

2 Mix in the milk and salt
and pour mixture into a
shallow pan. Dip in the bread.

3 Cook in hot fat. Turn to
brown on both sides. Add
confectioners' sugar, serve.

flip-flop pancakes

Produce a Paul Bunyan breakfast with lots of golden

pancakes. Of course, you'll have plenty of butter

ready and a pitcher of warm honey or syrup. But

some morning, try delicious Cranberry-Orange-Honey

Sauce for topping. Pancakes with the special sauce

also make a fine Sunday-night supper. Serve with

steaming mugs of coffee and tall glasses of milk.

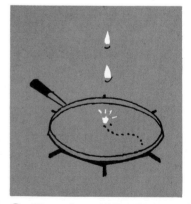

1 Look on the pancake-mix package. Find pancake recipe that uses eggs and shortening. Mix batter as directed.

2 Now, grease the griddle or skillet lightly with a little bit of shortening on a piece of folded waxed paper.

3 Heat the griddle. If drops of cold water skitter and dance around on griddle, it's hot enough to cook pancakes.

Make sky-high towers with cranberry sauce and pancakes. Dust top with confectioners' sugar.

You'll need:

Pancake mix   Milk

Eggs   Shortening

Take out:

bowl
measuring cups
wooden spoon
skillet or griddle
turner
potholder

4 Use ¼-cup measure when you pour batter onto the griddle. Measuring helps you keep all the pancakes the same size.

5 Pancakes get bubbly on top when they're ready to turn. Easy over! Lift with turner to see when second side is brown.

Special Cranberry-Orange-Honey Sauce

TAKE
1 1-pound can whole cranberry sauce
¼ cup orange juice
2 or 3 tablespoons honey (to suit your sweet tooth)

MIX them together very well

LADLE over pancakes — single or stacks

arty-surprise
SANDWICHES

You'll need:

2 3-ounce packages cream cheese	¼ cup milk	1 5-ounce can boned chicken	2 tablespoons mayonnaise
1 5-ounce jar pimiento-cheese spread	12 stuffed olives, chopped	18 slices bread crusts removed	Soft butter or margarine

Take out:

bowls
measuring cups
  and spoons
can opener
paring knife
bread knife
breadboard
table knife
small plates
salad forks

1 Soften cream cheese. Stir in milk gradually. Beat after adding milk.

2 Cut the chicken into small pieces. Put pieces into another bowl and add mayonnaise.

3 Put the cheese spread in a third bowl and stir in the olives with care.

4 Butter bread. Spread with chicken; add bread. Spread on olive-cheese; top with bread.

5 "Frost" with the softened cream cheese. Trim tops with olive "flowers." Chill.

You'll need:			Take out:
4 hard-cooked eggs	2 tablespoons chopped celery	1 tablespoon chopped green onion	covered saucepan paring knife cutting board measuring spoons bowls, spoon table knife wooden skewers potholder
2 tablespoons mayonnaise	1 tablespoon prepared mustard	¼ teaspoon salt	
4 unsliced coney buns	Soft butter or margarine	Leaf lettuce	

To cook eggs: Place eggs in pan. Cover with cold water. Heat slowly to boiling. Lower the heat. Cook over *very low* heat for 20 minutes.

Egg-salad
SANDWICH
BOATS

1 Cool cooked eggs in cold water—tap lightly to make crack. Then peel.
 After the shells are removed, chill.

2 Chop chilled eggs in bowl. Add celery, green onion, mustard, mayonnaise, and the salt. Mix all ingredients.

3 Hollow out tops of buns. Line hollows with leaf lettuce. Spoon in egg filling. Add paper-stick sails.

28

Egg in a bun sandwiches

Take out:

round biscuit cutter

fork

cooky sheet

potholders

turner

You'll need:

4 hamburger   4 eggs
buns

Soft butter   4 slices
or margarine cheese

Pepper   Salt

1 Set oven at 325°. Get the plates ready so you can whisk the sandwiches right to table.

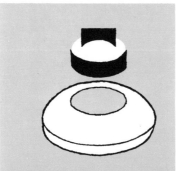

2 Put biscuit cutter in center of a bun. Cut down 1 inch. *Don't cut through bottom of bun.*

3 Carefully lift the circle out with a fork. Butter inside of bun well with butter or margarine.

4 Place buns on cooky sheet. Break an egg into each hole. Sprinkle with salt and pepper.

Cook egg before adding cheese

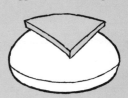

5 Place in oven. Bake 25 minutes. *Now* top with cheese slices. Bake about 5 more minutes.

Ideas for

a variety of breads and sandwiches that are speedy to fix, delicious

Dress up doughnuts for glamorous snacks or desserts. Use doughnuts from the bakery or market. One idea is to spread the rim of each doughnut with marshmallow cream and roll in chopped maraschino cherries. Or, spread doughnuts with peanut butter and roll in chopped peanuts. Softened cream cheese and chopped pecans taste good together, too. Spread cream cheese on doughnuts, dip in bowl of chopped pecans.

Peanut-butter S'mores: Split hamburger buns and spread each half with crunch-style peanut butter. Top with big dollop of marshmallow cream. Place the bun halves in the broiler and broil until the marshmallow topknot is lightly browned. Serve immediately.

Honey Butter turns pancakes (page 24) or French toast (page 23) into a treat. To make Honey Butter, mix together ½ cup butter or margarine and ¼ cup honey. Beat the mixture hard until it's all light and fluffy. Spoon it into bowl and serve at breakfast.

Pineapple Prize Pancakes are as easy as plain ones, but they'll earn you the "good cook" title. To make these pineapple treats, press 1 slice of well-drained pineapple into each circle of pancake batter on the griddle. Before the cake is ready to turn, hide the pineapple under a bit of batter. To do this, spoon on about 2 teaspoons of batter. Now flip the pancakes over and bake on the other side. Serve with warm syrup and lots of softened butter.

Cocoa Toast is a speedy breakfast specialty. Mix 3 tablespoons sugar, 1 tablespoon cocoa, ½ teaspoon cinnamon, and sprinkle over slices of hot, buttered toast.

Bread 'n butter sandwiches actually taste like something out of the ordinary when you fix them this way: Wrap the sandwiches in foil packages and put them in a 350° oven for about 10 minutes. The soft, buttery sandwiches will be so good they'll surprise you.

Salad-in-a-Sandwich: Spread one slice of toast with deviled ham, one slice with mayonnaise. Sandwich a lettuce leaf and four thin tomato slices in between the toast slices. Cut sandwich into quarters, serve with potato chips.

Garlic Bread goes with spaghetti (page 56) just like ice cream goes with cake. To fix Garlic Bread: Slice French bread in 1-inch slices, *without cutting through* bottom crust. Mix ½ cup soft butter or margarine with ¼ teaspoon garlic powder. Spread between slices of bread and over top of loaf. Wrap loaf in aluminum foil and heat in a 350° oven for 10 to 15 minutes. Serve in a basket or long bowl, using napkin or the foil to keep bread warm.

Grilled Cheese Sandwiches: For each sandwich, you'll need one slice process American cheese, two slices bread, and a tablespoon of butter or margarine. Put the cheese between bread slices. Melt butter in skillet. Toast the sandwich over low heat. Flip the sandwich with a turner so both sides can toast. Serve with a bowl of hot tomato soup.

Chapter 3

Candy and Cookies

Animal Cookies

Surprise your friends with a circus
parade of jaunty Animal Cookies,
lined up two-by-two. For a summertime
party, combine these special cookies
with tall glasses of chilly lemonade.
Tint the lemonade pink, using a drop or
two of red food coloring, and you'll
have a real circus-day party. A few
balloons would add to the festive look!

You'll need:	2 cups confectioners' sugar	2 tablespoons rich milk	Dash salt	½ teaspoon vanilla	Vanilla wafers	Animal crackers

Take out: sifter, waxed paper, measuring cups and spoons, turner, bowl, spoons

Animal Cookies could double as centerpiece for party table

These tasty cookies will make any party fun. It takes just a jiffy to fix the frosting and perch the animal crackers on their cooky bases. Count on your friends wanting lots of extras.

1   Sift confectioners' sugar onto waxed paper. Measure 2 cups. Put sugar in bowl.

2   Add milk, salt, vanilla; beat. Add tablespoon of milk if frosting is too stiff to spread.

3   Put wafers together with frosting. Stand a cracker in a dab on top.

Sugar drops

These crisp cookies are ready to eat in next to no time. They pack and mail well so are good to send to friends at Christmas.

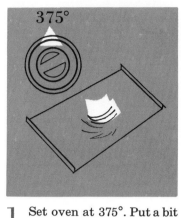

1 Set oven at 375°. Put a bit of shortening on waxed paper. Rub it over the cooky sheets till lightly greased.

You'll need:

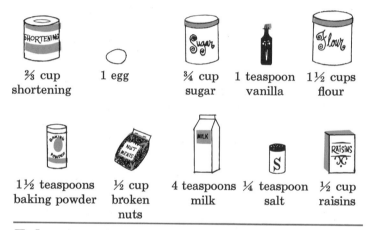

⅔ cup shortening   1 egg   ¾ cup sugar   1 teaspoon vanilla   1½ cups flour

1½ teaspoons baking powder   ½ cup broken nuts   4 teaspoons milk   ¼ teaspoon salt   ½ cup raisins

Take out:

measuring cups and spoons, mixing bowl, wooden spoon, flour sifter, waxed paper, two cooky sheets, cake rack, turner, potholder

2 Soften shortening with a wooden spoon. Mix sugar in thoroughly. Add egg. Beat until fluffy and unstreaked. Add vanilla and mix in well.

3 Sift flour. Then sift again with baking powder and salt onto waxed paper. Set aside until needed.

4 Add milk to shortening-egg mixture. Add flour mixture, nuts, and raisins. Stir. Drop by teaspoons on sheet.

Bake about 12 minutes

5 Bake about 12 minutes. Remove. Sprinkle on some sugar. While the first pan of cookies bakes, fix the next.

Raisin-oatmeal cookies

You'll need:

1 cup all-purpose flour	½ cup brown sugar	¼ cup granulated sugar	2 table-spoons milk	2 cups quick-cooking rolled oats	1 egg
1 cup raisins	½ teaspoon soda	½ teaspoon salt	1 teaspoon cinnamon	½ cup shortening	

1 Set oven at 375°. Lightly grease cooky sheets with little bit of shortening. Measure flour onto paper. Add soda, salt, and cinnamon and sift ingredients into a bowl.

Take out:

flour sifter, waxed paper, measuring cups and spoons, bowls, spatula, wooden spoon, cooky sheets, turner, rack, potholder

2 Add shortening, brown sugar, granulated sugar, egg, milk; mix well. Beat mixture hard; about 100 times.

3 Add raisins and oats. Drop teaspoons of cooky mixture 2 inches apart onto the greased cooky sheets and bake.

Bake about 12 minutes

4 Bake 12 to 15 minutes. Remove cookies from sheets with a turner. Place them on a cake rack to cool. Store in jar.

Honey-coconut bars

You'll need:

Pound cake

Coconut

Honey

Soft butter
or margarine

Take out:

bread knife

breadboard

table knife

cooky sheet

shallow pan

potholders

turner

1 Set oven at 375°. Take out cooky sheet and then grease it lightly, using bit of butter or margarine on a small piece of waxed paper. Set aside.

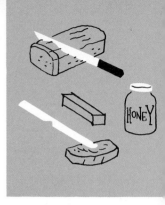

2 Cut the cake into 1-inch slices; cut each slice into three bars. Add butter, honey, on tops and sides of bars.

3 Put some coconut in shallow pan. Roll bars in the coconut until they're thoroughly covered on tops, sides.

4 Arrange bars on the cooky sheet; bake 5 to 10 minutes and remove them. Let cool.

Toasted coconut makes crisp "frosting"

Everyone likes
the good
taste of honey
combined
with coconut.

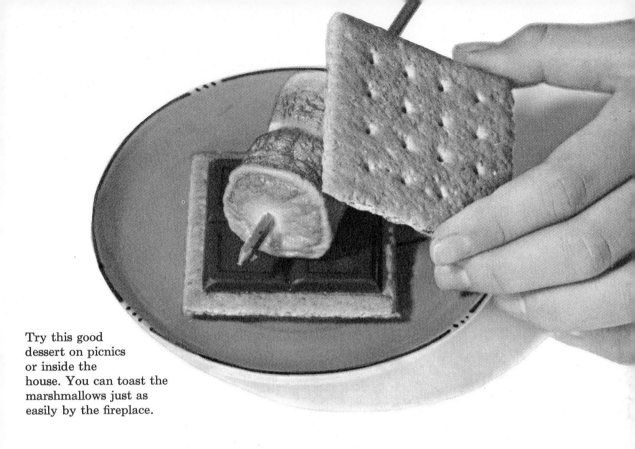

Try this good
dessert on picnics
or inside the
house. You can toast the
marshmallows just as
easily by the fireplace.

Picnic
some-mores

You'll need:

Marshmallows

Graham crackers

Flat bars of
milk chocolate

Take out:

long-handled
    fork or stick

plate

spoon

1 Toast double-header
(two marshmallows on
stick) slowly so marshmallows will be hot and gooey.

2 Top a cracker with
chocolate. Push the
marshmallows on, then,
top with cracker "lid."

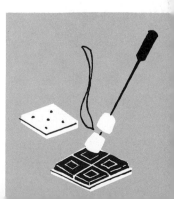

Yummy chocolate squares

You'll need:	Take out:
1 pound marshmallows	double boiler
1 cup broken walnuts	wooden spoon
3 tablespoons butter or margarine	8-inch square pan
1 cup crisp rice cereal	
½ teaspoon salt	rubber scraper
1 teaspoon vanilla	potholder
8 ounces semisweet chocolate	

1 Heat 2 inches of water in the bottom of double boiler. Grease square pan.

2 Melt marshmallows, butter, chocolate in double-boiler top. Take from heat.

3 Mix. Stir in rest of the ingredients. Spread in pan. Cut thirty-six pieces.

Caramel nut balls

You'll need:	1 cup chopped nuts
	2 tablespoons hot water
	½ pound caramels
	16 regular marshmallows
Take out:	double boiler, shallow pan, measuring cup and spoons, plate, wooden spoon, small spoon, skewer, potholder, waxed paper

1 Put nuts in pan. Butter plate. Boil water in the bottom of the double boiler.

2 Melt caramels with hot water in top of double boiler. Stir caramels well.

3 Dip the marshmallows into hot caramel sauce; then in nuts. Use a skewer.

Quick walnut panocha

1 Butter the pan very lightly. Sift and measure confectioners' sugar. Melt the butter.

2 Stir in brown sugar. Stir over low heat 2 minutes. Add the milk. Cook till boiling.

3 Cool. Beat in confectioners' sugar till candy looks like fudge. Add nuts. Pour in pan.

You'll need:

1 cup brown sugar
1¾ to 2 cups
   confectioners' sugar
½ cup butter
   or margarine
¼ cup milk
1 cup broken walnuts

Take out:

flour sifter
waxed paper
measuring cups
spatula
saucepan
wooden spoon
8-inch square pan
potholder

Stir all the time this candy cooks to make it good.

Creamy fudge

Take out:	double boiler	measuring spoons and cup	sifter waxed paper spoon	rubber scraper	8-inch square pan	bowl	paper towels
You'll need:	4 1-ounce squares unsweetened chocolate	2 3-ounce packages cream cheese	4 cups confectioners' sugar	½ teaspoon vanilla	Dash salt	½ cup chopped California walnuts	

1 Lightly butter 8-inch square pan. Put 2 inches water in double-boiler bottom. Bring to boil.

2 Melt 4 squares of chocolate in double-boiler top. Have the cheese at room temperature. Put cheese in a bowl.

3 Use wooden spoon to break up the cream cheese in the bowl. Rub cheese against the bowl; beat it until it is smooth and soft.

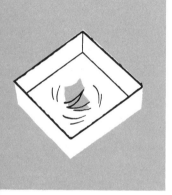

4 Slowly stir in sifted confectioners' sugar, salt. Work spoon carefully so sugar will stay in bowl.

5 Now add the melted chocolate. Use rubber scraper to get all of it out of pan. Mix well. Add vanilla, chopped nuts.

6 Press mixture into square pan. Chill in refrigerator till it is firm. Cut in squares. Top each piece with nut half if you wish.

Ideas for

making more kinds of candies and ready-in-a-hurry cookies

For delicious marshmallow candies by the plateful, start with the recipe for Caramel Nut Balls on page 36. Then, try the following variations of that easy recipe.

Chocolate Clouds: Melt a package of candy-dipping chocolate in the top of the double boiler. Melt this the same way you melted caramels for Caramel Nut Balls, page 36. Dip the marshmallows to coat with chocolate, roll them in chopped nuts. Place on a plate until the chocolate is cool and firm and then serve.

Glittery Sugar Mallows: Dunk marshmallows in a bowl of light cream. Then roll them in piles of colored sugar. This variation is especially nice for the plates of Christmas candies you fix.

Coconut Snowballs: First, roll marshmallows in slightly-beaten egg white. While they are still moist, roll them through a drift of fluffy coconut. Let the egg white-coconut mixture become firm.

Frozen cooky dough that you can buy at the market gives cooky-jar fillers a flying start. Choose from butterscotch, chocolate, oatmeal, or any other type of cooky that you like. Or, make two or three kinds to please everyone. Easy, easy cookies come from cooky mixes in boxes, too. Just follow the directions and bake the simple way they suggest.

Perky cooky faces are good partytime favors. These cooky faces start out as vanilla wafers that you buy in a box at the market. Sandwich two vanilla wafers with Confectioners' Icing: Mix ½ cup confectioners' sugar with enough milk to make icing spread nicely. Use a salted peanut half as a "topknot"; stick in icing. Ice front of cooky sandwich and add semisweet chocolate pieces for eyes.

Eat-right-away Cookies are fun because no one expects you to save any for tomorrow. Mix 2 tablespoons honey with ½ cup coconut. Spread on 12 salted crackers. Put on a cooky sheet and bake in a 375° oven for about 7 minutes. Take them from the oven when they're golden brown and then serve while they are still toasty and warm.

Caramel Snappers. For each piece you'll need 4 pecan halves, 1 caramel, and some melted semisweet chocolate pieces. Put a caramel on each cluster of pecans on a buttered baking sheet. Heat in a 325° oven for 4 to 8 minutes to soften the caramels. Remove from the oven.

    Mash softened caramels over the pecans with a buttered spatula. Let them cool. While they are cooling, melt the chocolate pieces. When the caramels have cooled, spoon some melted chocolate over each piece. Let the chocolate cool.

For Stuffed Dates, you'll need 1 tablespoon butter or margarine, 1¾ cups sifted confectioners' sugar, 2 tablespoons orange juice, and 1 6½-ounce package of pitted dates. Soften the butter with a spoon. Sift and measure sugar. Add to butter. Beat. Stir in orange juice. Make pencillike rolls out of the candy mixture. Cut short lengths of the rolls and stuff into each pitted date. Glistening jelly-string gumdrops make a pretty trim for the Stuffed Dates. Trim some of white-candy stuffings with red stripes, some with green and yellow.

Chapter 4

Desserts

Ice cream pops

You'll need:	Take out:
1 pint vanilla brick ice cream	sharp knife
	shallow pan
	measuring cups
4 wooden spoons	spoon
1 5-ounce bar milk chocolate	double boiler
	table knife
¼ cup shortening	

 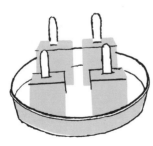  

1 Cut ice cream in two. Cut each piece again. Stick a spoon in each piece.

2 Put in pan and freeze. Put 2 inches water in bottom of double boiler.

3 Melt chocolate and shortening in top of double boiler, mixing well.

4 Let chocolate and shortening cool till warm. Spread on "pops." Freeze.

Yum*sicles*

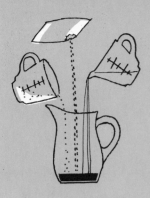

1 Put drink powder in pitcher. Add water and sugar. Stir with a spoon until dissolved.

You'll need:	Plastic spoons	1 package flavored summer-drink powder	4 cups water	¾ cup sugar
Take out:	pitcher, measuring cups, spoon, paper cups			

Make some fruit-flavored icicles for your playtime thirst-quenchers. If you have sucker molds, use them instead of paper cups.

2 Pour in paper cups. Put in the freezing compartment. Watch for it to get mushy.

3 When mixture gets mushy, stick in the plastic spoons. Freeze. Tear off cups to eat.

Baked apples

 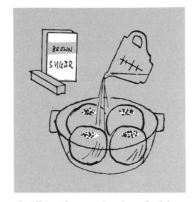 

1 Set the oven temperature indicator at 375°. Wash the apples thoroughly under running water. Dry them. Remove cores. Mother will show you how.

2 Put the apples in a baking dish. Pack the cores with brown sugar and butter. Then, pour water around the apples. Place a cover on baking dish.

3 Bake about 45 minutes. Test tenderness with a fork. If fork doesn't prick easily, put apples back in oven for baking.

You'll need:

4 apples
¼ cup
　brown sugar
2 teaspoons
　butter or
　margarine
1 cup water

Take out:

apple corer
covered baking
　dish
measuring cups
　and spoons
potholders

→
Sweet baked apples look pretty, taste good. They can be served cold or hot with lots of rich cream and sugar.

Applesauce with red hots

1 Wash apples. Cut them in quarters. Peel and core each. Slice into two or three pieces and place in saucepan.

2 Add water. Cover the pan. Cook apples slowly until tender. To test the tenderness, prick apple slice with a fork.

3 Remove from heat. Add red hots. They dissolve as you beat applesauce smooth with spoon. Serve hot or cold.

You'll need:	¼ cup water	4 tart apples	Bottle of red hots
Take out:	paring knife	covered saucepan	spoon potholder	measuring cup

To make natural-colored applesauce, you should leave out the red-hot candies and add ¼ cup of sugar to the recipe.

Easy lemon pie

You can serve this pie proudly. It's fancy
enough for a party but is so fast to fix.
Just for fun—design a special top trim.

Crumb crust

You'll need:	Take out:
14 graham crackers	clean paper sack or plastic bag
	rolling pin
	measuring cups
¼ cup sugar	small skillet
	mixing bowl
	spoon
6 tablespoons butter or margarine	8-inch pieplate

Lemon filling

You'll need:	Take out:
1 egg	small bowl
	fork
1 teaspoon grated lemon peel	grater
	waxed paper
½ cup lemon juice	measuring spoons and cups
	juicer
1 15-ounce can sweetened condensed milk	mixing bowl
	spoon
	can opener

Crumb crust

1 Put crackers in a sack. Roll with a rolling pin. Measure.

2 Put 1¼ cups of crumbs into a mixing bowl. Add the sugar. Mix the crumbs, sugar well.

3 Melt butter in the skillet. Stir into crumb mixture and press in piepan. Chill 45 minutes.

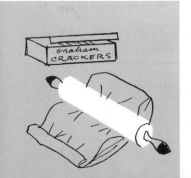

Lemon filling

1 Break egg into small bowl. Beat with fork until no egg white shows.

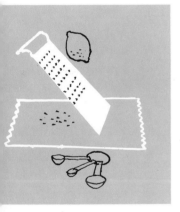

2 Grate lemon peel on waxed paper. (Be careful of fingers!) Measure the peel after you grate.

Save some crumb mixture to make circle topping. Or, design another topping.

3 Now cut the lemons in half. Squeeze in juicer till you have ½ cup.

4 Place milk in bowl. Add the egg, lemon peel, and juice. Stir until the mixture thickens.

5 Spread lemon filling in the pie shell. Chill the pie about 1 hour or till it is firm.

Chocolate-peppermint delicious

Take out:

plastic or paper bags, rolling pin, bowl, egg beater, refrigerator tray, spoon

You'll need:

2 ounces peppermint stick candy, ½ of 8-ounce box chocolate wafers, 1 cup whipping cream

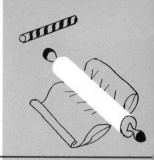

1 Put candy into bag. Roll with a rolling pin until crumbs form in bag.

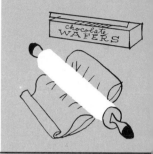

2 Put the cookies into a second plastic bag or paper sack. Roll cookies with rolling pin until they are thoroughly crushed.

3 Whip cream and add the candy crumbs and the cooky crumbs. Stir gently to mix and freeze in refrigerator. Serves 8.

Chocolate refrigerator dessert

Take out:

mixing bowl, egg beater, measuring cups and spoons, large plate, table knife

You'll need:

1½ cups whipping cream, 2 teaspoons confectioners' sugar, ½ teaspoon vanilla, 30 chocolate wafers, California walnut halves

1 Beat the cream till it's fluffy. Add sugar and vanilla and beat well. The cream is ready when it will stand in little peaks.

2 Spread a cooky with the whipped cream mixture. Spread second cooky with mixture and stack it on the first as shown.

3 Continue arranging the cookies; put five in each stack —on top, add some whipped cream, a nut.

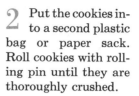

Date-marshmallow log

Take out:	paper sack or plastic bag, rolling pin, scissors, bowl, measuring cups, waxed paper
You'll need:	30 graham crackers, 16 marshmallows, 1 cup chopped dates, 2 cups broken walnuts, 1 cup whipping cream

1 Put graham crackers in a sack or bag. Fold back the edge. Crush crackers fine with rolling pin. Put them in bowl.

This super-rich dessert is a good one to choose if you want to have it done long before dinner.

2 Cut each marshmallow in 4 pieces. Wet scissors between cuts to prevent sticking. Put pieces in bowl with crumbs.

3 Cut the dates into bits; measure 1 cup. Add to the crumbs-marshmallows. Break the walnuts if necessary; measure 2 cups. Add the nuts.

4 Mix in the cream. Note: it is *not* whipped first. When cream is blended in thoroughly, turn mixture out on waxed paper. Shape into 3-inch roll.

5 Wrap roll in waxed paper and chill in the refrigerator for several hours or overnight. Cut into 8 slices to serve.

1 Put tapioca, sugar, salt, grape juice in a saucepan. Mix well.

2 Cook and stir over medium heat till mixture boils. Stir in the lemon juice. Cool.

3 After 20 minutes, stir the pudding. Spoon into dessert dishes. Chill then serve.

Grape tapioca

You'll need:	¼ cup quick-cooking tapioca
	¼ cup sugar 2½ cups grape juice
	Dash salt 1 tablespoon lemon juice
Take out:	measuring spoons and cups
	saucepan wooden spoon
	potholder dessert dishes

Candy-top cake

You'll need:	1 package yellow cake mix	1 6-ounce package semisweet chocolate pieces	½ cup broken California walnuts
Take out:	mixing bowl	measuring cups	wooden spoon	square cake pan
	paper	pencil	scissors	rubber spatula
	potholders	toothpicks	cake rack	narrow spatula

1 Set oven at temperature given on the package. Get pan out. Mix cake and bake as directed.

2 When cake is done, remove it from oven. Leave in pan and put on cake rack. Sprinkle chocolate pieces over the top of the hot cake at once.

3 When the chocolate is completely melted, spread it over cake with a narrow spatula. Sprinkle top of cake with nuts. Let cool. Cut in squares. Serve.

Ideas for

making quick desserts that are extra tasty and easy dessert trims

Have you ever tasted a Doughnut Sundae? To fix this treat, split the doughnuts in halves like hamburger buns. Place each of the bottom halves on separate dessert plates. Cover the bottom halves with big scoops of butter-pecan ice cream. Then, add the doughnut "lids" on the tops. Drizzle the sundaes with Hopscotch Butterscotch Sauce that you make like this:

Mix together: 3 tablespoons melted butter or
margarine
½ cup brown sugar
¼ cup light cream
Simmer 5 minutes. Beat ½ minute. It's ready to serve.
Make the butterscotch sauce before you start to assemble the Doughnut Sundaes on the plates.

Slick-trick desserts: Turn any flavor of pudding into a graham-cracker pie crust that is explained on page 44. Or, for a pudding-type dessert, cut four fig-bar cookies into quarters. Place in dessert dish. Pour light cream over them; add a maraschino cherry top.

In the springtime, hop a parade of Marshmallow Bun-Rabbits around a partytime cake. First, bake a yellow or white cake, following the directions given on the cake-mix package. Frost with a white frosting mix. Or, tint frosting yellow with a little yellow food coloring if you wish. Then, make a "bunny" favor for each of the guests you have invited to the party. You might make a few extras to place around the cake plate.

Use a toothpick to fasten two marshmallows together. Use a piece of toothpick to fasten on a marshmallow quarter for a tail. Cut the bunny ears from stiff pink construction paper. Poke ears into the top marshmallow. Then, very carefully paint the face on the Marshmallow Bun-Rabbit. Dip a toothpick in red food coloring and draw on the "dot" eyes and a smiling mouth. Add yellow "whiskers."

Ice-cream Sandwiches—so good! Cut a brick of peppermint ice cream into 4 slices. Sandwich each between 2 graham crackers. Let everyone pour on his own Glossy Fudge Sauce. This is fork food. To make the rich fudge sauce in a hurry:

Mix together: 1 cup instant cocoa
⅛ cup boiling water
1 tablespoon butter
Use right away while hot, or let it cool and thicken.

For a lacy design on a cake: Instead of frosting a cake, place a paper doily on top of cake; sift confectioners' sugar lightly and evenly over the doily. Now, carefully lift off the doily. The lacy design of the sugar makes a pretty topping for special occasions.

Hot Chocolate-Peppermint Sundae: For a half cup of sauce, you'll need 12 chocolate-covered fondant-filled mint patties and 2 tablespoons cream. Melt mints in top of a double boiler. Remove and add cream. Stir. Spoon warm sauce over scoops of vanilla ice cream.

Chapter **5**

Main dishes

Frankfurters

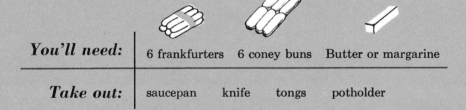

You'll need: | 6 frankfurters | 6 coney buns | Butter or margarine

Take out: | saucepan | knife | tongs | potholder

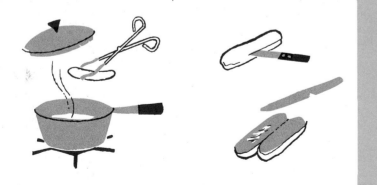

1 Half fill pan with water. Bring to boil; add franks. Cover the saucepan and let the water return to boil. At once, remove pan from heat. Put on hot pad.

2 Let franks stand for 8 to 10 minutes. During this time, butter the buns. Put franks in buns, using tongs to handle them. Add mustard, catsup, or relish.

Saucy Franks

You'll need: ½ cup chopped onion, 1 tablespoon fat, 1 14-ounce bottle catsup, ¼ cup of water, 1 tablespoon vinegar, 1 tablespoon sugar, ¼ cup pickle relish, ¼ teaspoon salt, dash pepper, 8 to 10 frankfurters, 8 to 10 buns. Heat electric skillet to 250°. Cook onion in fat, add other ingredients except the buns. Set heat at 220°. Cover. Simmer 15 minutes.

Hamburgers

1 Measure ⅓ cup of beef for each patty. Make 6 of the patties.

2 Brown meat patties on both sides in skillet over medium heat.

3 Sprinkle with salt and pepper. Serve them in buttered buns.

You'll need:	1 pound ground beef, salt and pepper, 6 hamburger buns, butter or margarine
Take out:	knife, skillet, measuring spoons and cup, turner, potholder

Add a tomato slice and cheese slice to each and broil a few minutes.

BAR-B-Q-burgers

You'll need: 1 pound ground beef, ⅔ cup of chopped onion, ½ teaspoon salt, dash pepper, ¼ cup of water, 1 10½-ounce can condensed chicken gumbo soup, 1 tablespoon catsup, and 1 tablespoon prepared mustard.

Take out: skillet, paring knife, measuring cups and spoons, can opener, wooden spoon, potholder.

Cook the meat and onion together until the meat is lightly browned. Stir frequently with a wooden spoon.

Add the other ingredients. Cover; simmer over *low* heat gently for 30 minutes. Stir occasionally. When barbecued mixture is done, spoon into eight buns. Serve at once.

Oven-fried chicken

You'll need:

½ cup butter or
  margarine
1 4-ounce
  package potato chips
¼ teaspoon garlic salt
Dash pepper
1 2½- or 3-
  pound ready-to-
  cook broiler-
  fryer chicken, cut up

Take out:

jellyroll pan
rolling pin
waxed paper
measuring cups
  and spoons
skillet
potholders

1 Set oven control temperature at 375°. Melt butter
in a small skillet.

2 Crush potato chips with rolling pin before opening. Mix
chips with garlic salt, pepper.

3 Dip chicken in melted butter,
roll in potato-chip mixture.
Keep the mixture on waxed paper.

4 Place pieces on pan—
skin side up. Pour rest
butter, crumbs over. Bake.

Bake 1 hour without turning.→
The recipe will serve four.

Scalloped salmon

You'll need:	1 7¾-ounce can salmon	About 40 single saltine crackers	6 tablespoons butter or margarine, melted	1 tablespoon chopped onion	1 cup milk	Dash pepper

Take out:	can opener mixing bowls measuring cups and spoons 8-inch piepan fork skillet potholders paper or plastic bag spoon rolling pin paring knife

1 Set oven temperature at 400°. This recipe will serve four or five people.

2 Open can of salmon. Pour off liquid. Put salmon in a bowl. Flake it with a fork.

3 Crush saltines in a bag with a rolling pin (not too fine). Measure 2 cups crumbs.

Mushroom Sauce

1 10½-ounce can condensed cream of mushroom soup
⅛ cup milk

Mix soup and milk together in a saucepan. Cook and stir over medium heat until the sauce is smooth and hot. Serve with Scalloped salmon.

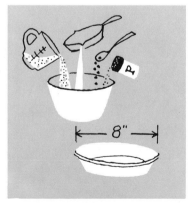

4 Combine saltines, butter, onion, pepper in bowl. Put ⅓ of mixture in piepan.

5 Spoon in half the salmon. Repeat and cover with last ⅓ of crumbs. Add milk. Bake.

Everyday drumsticks

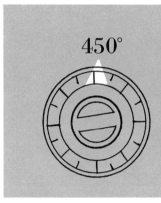

450°

1 First step is set oven at 450°. This recipe will serve six.

You'll need:	1 pound ground beef	1 teaspoon salt	1 egg
	12 soda crackers	6 wooden skewers	3 slices bacon
Take out:	mixing bowl, wooden spoon, paper or plastic bag, rolling pin, waxed paper, baking pan, kitchen scissors, potholders, turner		

Everyone likes mock drumsticks

2 Put ground beef, salt, egg in bowl. Stir gently, thoroughly. Divide into six parts.

3 Put crackers in bag and roll with a rolling pin. Place crumbs on waxed paper.

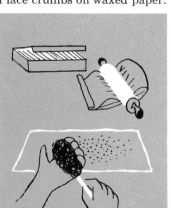

4 Shape meat mix around skewers. Roll in crumbs. Put in a greased baking pan.

5 Bake 15 minutes. Add bacon slices. Bake 15 minutes.

Bake 15 minutes. Add bacon; return to oven

Minute steps

1 Wait to cook the juicy steaks till the rest of the meal is ready. You could garnish steak platter with tiny onions.

First, melt fat in skillet over moderate heat. Put in steaks.

You'll need:	Take out:
 1 tablespoon fat Minute steaks Salt Pepper	spoon skillet turner or tongs potholder

2 Cook one to two minutes on one side. Turn. Brown on the other side. Check occasionally to see how the steaks are browning. Sprinkle with salt and pepper. Remove with turner or tongs. Serve.

You'll need:

1 can
spaghetti in tomato
sauce with cheese

1 4-ounce can
Vienna sausage

Take out:

saucepan, skillet,
can opener, spoon,
fork, serving dish,
potholder

SAUCY spaghetti

1 Open can of spaghetti;
empty the contents into
saucepan. Heat slowly. Stir
occasionally with a spoon.

2 Open can of Vienna sausage
and put sausages in a skillet. Heat slowly over low heat.
Use fork to turn the sausages.

3 Arrange the hot spaghetti
and the sausage on serving
plate. Serve with grated Parmesan cheese. Serves two or three.

You'll need:

1 7¼-ounce package macaroni-and-cheese dinner	6 cups water	3 tablespoons butter or margarine	2 teaspoons salt	¼ cup milk	1 sprig parsley

Take out:

big pan	measuring spoons	potholder
spoon	and cup	fork
large sieve	serving dish	

Macaroni and cheese

1 Put water and salt in big pan; heat to boiling. (You know the water is boiling when it bubbles and "rolls" in pan.)

2 Add macaroni to boiling water. (Save out package of cheese.) Stir. Let water return to boil for 7 minutes.

3 *Carefully* pour water and the macaroni into a sieve. Do this over the sink. Be careful not to get burned by the hot steam.

4 Put the hot macaroni in a serving dish. Add butter, milk, and cheese from the envelope to macaroni.

5 Mix *quickly* till butter and cheese melt and are creamy. Add parsley. Serve at once. Makes four servings.

Super soup

You'll need:

1 can condensed cream of chicken soup

1 can condensed vegetable-beef soup

1 can milk

1 can water

Take out:

can opener

saucepan

spoon

potholder

1 Open the two cans of soup and pour contents of both into deep saucepan. Stir them gently till they're well mixed.

2 Fill one can with milk and the other can with water. Pour each gradually into pan. Stir mixture well as you pour.

3 Heat just to boiling—do not let soups boil. Garnish with parsley and pimiento if you wish. Makes 4 to 5 servings.

MAGIC
white-sauce supper

To white sauce, add 4 sliced, hard-cooked eggs, ½ cup peas. Heat. Serve over hot biscuits.

1 Place 1 or 2 inches water in the bottom of a double boiler. Heat to boiling, then, set the heat so water simmers.

You'll need:

2 tablespoons butter or margarine	2 tablespoons flour	1 cup milk	¼ teaspoon salt	Dash pepper

Take out:

double boiler, wooden spoon, measuring cups and spoons, potholder

2 Put butter in the top of the double boiler. Place it over hot water. Heat until the butter melts. Then, stir in flour.

3 Add milk slowly. Stir all the time. Cook until the white sauce is thick and very smooth. Stir sauce constantly.

Cook for 7 minutes

4 Next stir in the salt and pepper. Put on the cover of pan and cook sauce over hot water 7 minutes.

Speedy chili

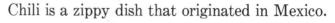

Chili is a zippy dish that originated in Mexico. When you serve chili, pass a basket of crisp crackers. This recipe will make six servings.

You'll need:

½ cup chopped onion

¼ cup chopped green pepper

1 pound ground beef

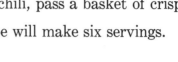

2 8-ounce cans (2 cups) tomato sauce

1 1-pound can (2 cups) kidney beans

1 teaspoon salt

Chili powder

Take out:

measuring cups and spoons
paring knife
big saucepan
wooden spoon
can opener
potholder

1 Cook onion, pepper, and beef together in a pan till the meat is lightly browned.

Cook about 5 minutes

2 Add tomato sauce; cook on low heat 5 minutes. Add the kidney beans, salt. Heat.

3 Stir in 1 teaspoon chili powder. Taste. Add a little more if you like.

Fluffy scrambled eggs

Bacon is easy when it's cooked this way. Place the bacon strips in a cold skillet. Set the heat low and COOK very slowly. TURN pieces with tongs. When bacon is as done as you like it, remove it from the skillet. As the bacon cools, it gets crisper. Put strips on paper towels to DRAIN off extra fat. Towels also help bacon stay piping hot.

You'll need:

6 eggs ⅛ cup light cream ¾ teaspoon salt Dash pepper

Take out: mixing bowl, measuring spoons and cup, egg beater, wooden spoon, double boiler, potholder

1 Put two inches of water in bottom of the double boiler. Heat the water to boiling.

2 Break eggs into bowl. Beat smooth so no white shows. Add cream, salt, and pepper.

3 Cook in top of double boiler. Stir occasionally. This makes four servings.

Stuffed eggs

Arrange Stuffed Eggs on a plate
and serve with sandwiches at lunch.

Or, let eggs travel to a picnic.

You'll need:

6 eggs

2 tablespoons mayonnaise

1 teaspoon vinegar

1 teaspoon prepared mustard

½ teaspoon salt

Dash pepper

¼ teaspoon paprika

Take out:
covered saucepan
paring knife
small bowl
measuring spoons
plate and spoon
potholder

Cook about 20 minutes

1 Put eggs in pan. Cover with cold water. Heat to boiling. Lower heat; cook over *very low heat* 20 minutes.

2 Cool the eggs in cold water. Then, tap them lightly all over to make them crack, and peel under cold running water.

3 Carefully cut the eggs in half lengthwise. Remove the yolks and put them in small bowl. Put the whites aside till later.

4 Mash yolks. Stir in mayonnaise, vinegar, mustard, salt, pepper, paprika. Stir till smooth. Spoon yolks into whites.

Ideas for

setting a pretty and proper table and for easy appetizers to serve

The good food you cook will look even better when it's served in an attractive way. Another important reason for proper table settings—they make eating much more convenient.

The silver and plate go one inch from the edge of the table. This placement keeps them safe from accidental "bumps." If Father serves at your house, the plates belong in a stack at his place.

Arrange silverware in the order you use it, from the outside in. The knives and spoons are on the right and the forks on the left. This way, you don't have to change hands when you pick them up.

The knife blade turns toward the plate because then it's ready to pick up.

The cup and saucer and tumbler go on the right as is shown in the drawing.

Napkins go beside the forks if you don't have a salad plate. Put the fold away from the plate. In case the table looks crowded, put the napkin right on the dinner plate. Just one more thing: Serving dishes and salt and pepper shakers should go parallel to the edge of the table, never cater-cornered. This makes the table setting more pleasing to the eye.

Appetizers or starters are not absolutely necessary, but they are a nice addition to a meal. You'll want to start your party meals with one, and, special family meals too. These foods aren't meant to fill you up. They're just to make you hungry for the delicious foods you plan to serve next. Among the appetizers and starters, you may choose from:

1. A small glass of tomato juice with a lemon wedge slipped over the rim. Easy, and good too.

2. A juice glass of pineapple juice with a tiny scoop of lime ice in it. Keep the juice well chilled until serving time. Take ice from the freezer and add it at the last minute.

3. A small grapefruit half (cut around each section, please). Serve the grapefruit topped with a small spoonful of raspberry sherbet. Add the sherbet quickly and serve at once.

4. A cup of bouillon. Either heat a can of soup or make it from bouillon cubes. Before you serve this, top each cup with chopped chives or a paper-thin slice of lemon or lime.

5. Try jellied consomme in the summer. Chill a can of consomme in the refrigerator for at least 4 hours. To serve, spoon into bowls. Break into sparkling chunks with a fork.

6. Heat canned vegetable-juice cocktail and stir in butter—1 teaspoon for each cup. Serve.

7. Freeze ginger ale to a mush in refrigerator tray. Serve in chilled sherbets; top with chilled drained canned fruit cocktail. Or, pour ginger ale over chilled fruit cocktail.

64

Chapter 6

Salads and Vegetables

Banana-roll salad

Take out: two salad plates, knife

You'll need:

Lettuce leaves   1 banana   Mayonnaise   ¼ cup broken walnuts   8 canned grapefruit sections

1 Wash lettuce. Shake off water. Pat dry with paper towels. Put on salad plates.

2 Cut peeled banana in half. Place half on each plate. Spread each with mayonnaise.

3 Sprinkle with nuts and arrange the grapefruit sections around bananas.

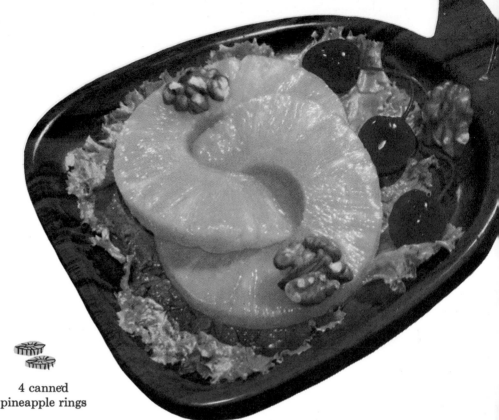

You'll need:

Lettuce leaves

4 canned
pineapple rings

Maraschino
cherries

Walnut halves

Take out: two salad plates
paring knife

Pineapple
double ring

1 Wash the lettuce leaves, and shake off the extra water. Arrange lettuce on the plates.

2 Cut through one side of pineapple ring. Slip another ring through. Place on lettuce.

3 Put on cherries and nuts as shown and serve with salad dressing. Makes two servings.

Grape surprise salad

You'll need:

 1 3-ounce package cream cheese

 2 tablespoons milk

 1 cup Tokay grapes

 Lettuce leaves

 6 canned pear halves

Take out: small bowl, fork, measuring spoons and cup, table knife, six salad plates

1 Put cheese in a bowl. Mash with fork. Stir in milk. Beat until smooth.

2 Pull grapes off stems. Wash them well. Cut in half. Use knife point to carefully remove the seeds.

3 Place washed lettuce on 6 plates. Put pear, the round side up, on each —spread cheese over pears.

4 Stick grape halves all over cheese on pears. Now the pear salads look like clusters of grapes.

Peter Rabbit salad

You'll need:	***Take out:***
Lettuce leaves	salad plates
Cloves	scissors
Canned pear halves	
Maraschino cherries	
Marshmallows	

1 Wash and dry the lettuce leaves. Put on plates. Place a pear, round side up, in the center of each plate.

2 Use marshmallow bits for ears, tails. Nose is a bit of cherry. Eyes are whole cloves.

Molded fruit salad

You'll need:	1 package lime-flavored gelatin	1 cup boiling water	1 No. 2 can (2½ cups) pineapple tidbits	2 medium bananas
Take out:	loaf pan, spoon, measuring cup, can opener, bowl, sieve, paring knife			

1 Put lime-flavored gelatin in loaf pan with a cup of boiling water and stir to dissolve the gelatin.

2 Open can of pineapple. Pour syrup and all into gelatin mixture. Stir. Pineapple will sink to bottom.

3 Peel the bananas. Then, slice them crosswise in circles; add to the gelatin. Chill the gelatin till firm.

Stack-up fruit salad

You'll need:

Lettuce leaves or endive

4 pineapple slices

4 peach halves

2 teaspoons peach syrup

4 maraschino cherries

¼ cup salad dressing or mayonnaise

Take out:

four salad plates

small bowl

measuring spoons

spoon

1 Wash, dry lettuce. Place on salad plates. Place pineapple slice on each. Top each with a peach half.

2 Mix salad dressing, peach syrup. Spoon in centers of peach halves. Top salads with cherries.

French-fried potatoes

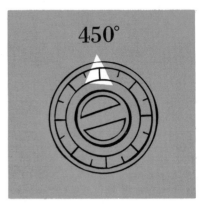

1 Set oven indicator at 450°. Take out the serving bowl or basket and line with a napkin.

You'll need: Take out:

1 package frozen French fries

 Salt

shallow pan

serving bowl

potholder

2 Spread frozen French fries out in a shallow pan. Put in the oven; bake 15 to 20 minutes.

French-fried potatoes go well with big, juicy hamburgers or frankfurters. Or, you can serve them with almost any main dish of meat.

3 Place in serving bowl or basket. Sprinkle with salt. Serve immediately. Serves 3 to 4.

Baked potatoes

For extra-mealy potatoes, roll them in your hands before you cut them open.

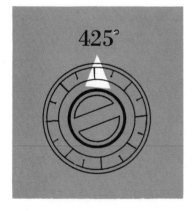

425°

1 Set oven at 425°. You will not need a pan. Just put potatoes on rack of the oven.

You'll need:

Baking potatoes

Butter or margarine

Take out:

vegetable brush
paring knife
fork
potholder
paper towels

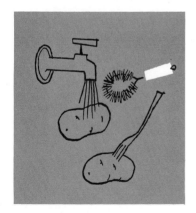

2 Wash off all of dirt. Stick with a fork to make holes for the hot steam to escape.

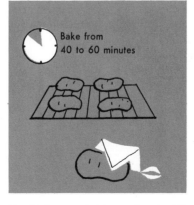

Bake from 40 to 60 minutes

3 Bake potatoes about 60 minutes. They'll be soft when squeezed with paper towel.

4 Cut a cross in the top of each potato. Stick a pat of soft butter in each opening.

Sunny carrots

You'll need:

Carrots Water Salt

Pepper Butter or margarine

Take out:
vegetable parer
paring knife
covered saucepan
fork

1 Wash carrots and pare with vegetable parer. When carrots are pared, use knife to cut them into long strips.

2 Put 1 inch cold water in pan. Salt till it tastes pleasantly salty. Bring to a boil. Add carrots and cover. Cook them about 15 minutes.

3 Test for tenderness, using a fork. When carrots are tender, drain. Put in a bowl. Season to taste with salt and pepper. Add a pat of butter on top and serve.

Scalloped tomatoes

You'll need:

| 3 slices toast | 1 1-pound can (2 cups) tomatoes | 1 tablespoon chopped onion | 1 teaspoon salt | ¼ cup butter or margarine |

Take out: can opener, knife, cutting board, measuring spoons and cups, 1-quart casserole, potholders, paper towels, small skillet

1 First of all, set the temperature indicator on the oven at 375°.

2 Cut the toast into small squares as shown. Cut on wood block or cutting board.

3 Peel onion. Cut two or three slices. Now chop it thoroughly and measure one tablespoon.

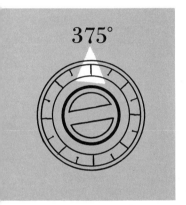  

4 Put layer of tomatoes in casserole. Add layer of toast. Continue adding the layers. Then, make a toast top. Sprinkle on salt, onion.

5 Place the butter or margarine in small skillet. Heat gently over low heat to melt. Pour evenly over the layers of toast and tomatoes.

6 Bake the casserole about 20 minutes. This casserole will serve four to five people. Take casserole directly to table. Use hot pad to protect the table.

Tuna salad

You'll need:

2 eggs
1 6½- or 7-
  ounce can
  tuna, flaked
½ cup
  chopped
  celery
¼ cup
  chopped
  cucumber
2 sweet
  pickles,
  chopped
Dash salt
Juice of
  ½ lemon
Mayonnaise
Lettuce

Take out:

can opener
bowl
saucepan
spoon
measuring
  cups
paring knife
fruit juicer
potholder

1 To hard-cook eggs, put in pan, cover with water. Heat to boiling. Cook over *very low* heat 20 minutes. Remove from hot water at once. Put eggs in cold water.

2 To peel eggs, tap so shells are covered with cracks. Roll gently between hands—peel under running water. When they are peeled, chop the eggs into a bowl.

3 Add tuna, celery, cucumber, pickle, salt, and lemon juice to egg. Add mayonnaise to moisten; toss. Chill. Line serving bowl with lettuce. Spoon in salad.

Cook about
20 minutes

1 Cook potatoes in their jackets about 20 minutes or until a fork pricks easily. Let cool. Hard-cook eggs as explained in Tuna Salad above. Cool the eggs, crack and peel them. Peel potatoes.

2 Slice the eggs and potatoes into the bowl. Add celery, green onions, cucumber, salt, French dressing. Chill the salad for 4 to 6 hours. At serving time, add enough mayonnaise to moisten. Garnish it with wedges of tomato.

Potato salad

You'll need:

6 potatoes
3 hard-cooked eggs
1 cup chopped
  celery
2 tablespoons
  chopped green
  onions
1 cucumber chopped
1½ teaspoons salt
¼ cup French
  dressing
Mayonnaise

Take out:

2 covered
  saucepans
measuring cups
  and spoons
bowl
paring knife
potholder
spoon

T🍅mat🍅
sandwich salad

You'll need:	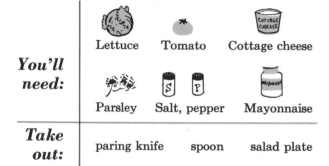		
	Lettuce	Tomato	Cottage cheese
	Parsley	Salt, pepper	Mayonnaise
Take out:	paring knife	spoon	salad plate

A summertime salad supreme! Serve with cold mayonnaise.

1 Wash lettuce leaves; shake off water. Arrange leaves on plate.

2 Wash tomato. Cut in thirds. Put the bottom piece on lettuce.

3 Top with layer of cottage cheese. Add little salt and pepper.

4 Add another tomato slice; more cheese; tomato; parsley sprig.

Pretty relish tray

You'll need:	Radishes	Green onions	Ice
Take out:	paring knife	bowl	
	serving tray or plate		

Roses. Wash radishes. Take off tops. For a rose, mark petals—start at end away from stem. Cut the petals.

Accordions. Cut radishes crosswise in about 10 or 12 narrow slices. Don't cut completely through.

Dominoes. Cut a deep "X" at tip of each radish. Slice off a circle in the center of each of "fourths."

Daisies. Cut 5 deep slices each way in a half radish. Soak radishes, clean onions in ice water. Serve.

Tossed green salad

You'll need:	Take out:
½ head lettuce	salad bowl
2 tablespoons sliced green onions	paring knife
¼ cup sliced radishes	measuring cups and spoons
⅓ cup chopped celery	salad fork and spoon
2 tomatoes	
¼ cup French dressing	

1 *Break* lettuce into salad bowl. Use fingers. Add onion, radishes, and celery.

2 Wash tomatoes. Cut out the stem ends. Slice in wedges. Add to salad bowl.

3 Pour dressing over the salad. Toss with a big fork, spoon. Serves four.

Ideas for

cooking vegetables the correct way so they'll taste just right

You can serve vegetables with all kinds of fix-ups, but unless they are cooked properly they'll never taste as good as they could. Here are the simple rules for vegetable cooking. If you follow these suggestions, your vegetables will be perfect every time.

Canned vegetables. These are already cooked so all you do is heat them before serving. To heat, open can, pour liquid, but not vegetables, into a saucepan. Hold saucer over open end of can to keep vegetables inside while you're pouring. Boil away part of the liquid in the saucepan. Add the vegetables and sprinkle with salt and pepper and add a butter pat if you wish. Heat until the vegetables are warm clear through. Serve.

Frozen vegetables. Directions on the package will be your biggest help with these. They will tell you just how to prepare the food. All kinds of frozen vegetables cook quickly.

Fresh vegetables. Printed directions don't come with these, but here's what you want to remember when you're cooking fresh vegetables:
1. Wash the vegetables thoroughly. Scrub them if they need it. You'll want the whole panful of vegetables to get done at the same time, so cut them into pieces of the same size. Cut on a wood cutting board and watch the fingers!
2. How much water you'll need to use is the first thing to decide. You don't want to float all the vitamins and minerals away, but neither do you want burned vegetables. Ask Mother to help you judge how much water you need.
3. Vegetable flavors are nicer when you cook vegetables in salted water. Add salt to the *cold* water so you can taste to tell when it's pleasantly salty (this takes about ½ teaspoon to 1 cup of water).
4. Bring *water* to boil.
5. *Now* put in the vegetables; add the pan cover.
6. Wait for a minute or so and peek under the cover once in awhile. You start counting cooking time when the water starts to boil again.
7. Turn down the heat so the vegetables just boil gently. If the heat is too high, vegetables may boil over or cook dry before they're done. Vegetables are done when they're *just* tender. The table below gives you an idea of how long this will take. Limp, soggy vegetables aren't good and they aren't as good for you. Either test with a fork or take a little piece from the pan. Taste it. Does it "chew" the way that you like it? If so, the cooking time is over.
8. Nobody likes cold vegetables unless they're supposed to be that way. Lift the cooked vegetables from the pan with a slotted spoon and serve at once.

Vegetable cooking times

Asparagus...............10 to 15 minutes	Cauliflower, flowerets.....10 to 15 minutes
Beans, green or wax.......15 to 30 minutes	Corn on the cob..........6 to 8 minutes
Beets, whole, young......35 to 60 minutes	Onions.................25 to 35 minutes
Broccoli.................10 to 20 minutes	Peas, green..............8 to 15 minutes
Brussels sprouts.........10 to 15 minutes	Potatoes, whole or
Cabbage, young,	halves................25 to 40 minutes
shredded..............5 to 7 minutes	Rutabagas...............25 to 40 minutes
wedges...........10 to 12 minutes	Spinach.................3 to 5 minutes
Carrots, young,	Tomatoes, cut up........10 to 15 minutes
slices or strips.........15 to 20 minutes	Turnips, sliced..........15 to 20 minutes

Meal plans

Sunday breakfast

—by you

Chilled Orange Juice
French Toast (*page 23*)
Confectioners' Sugar, Syrup, Jelly, Butter
Bacon Strips (*page 61*)
Milk　　　　　　　**Coffee**

Let your mother be the lazybones some Sunday morning, you be the early bird. Ask Dad if he'd turn out in time to make a pot of coffee for you. Set the table first and round up all the good things that you are going to serve with the French Toast.

If you have time, the family will thank you for warming the syrup. Ask Mother how she wants you to do that. Sift the sugar so it won't have any lumps or, better yet, serve it in a big shaker.

When the bacon's crisp, drain it on paper towels and cover it with more paper towels to keep it warm.

While toast gets brown and beautiful, (in the same skillet you fried bacon), give your folks a cup of Dad's coffee to sip as they browse the morning paper.

Lightning lunch

Super Soup (*page 58*)
Peanut Butter-Honey Sandwiches
Shoestring Potatoes
Shiny Red Apples
Raisin-Oatmeal Cookies (*page 33*)

When a situation calls for a fast feast, you're just the cook to whip it up. And nothing dull about it, either. The trick is to put two kinds of canned soup together to make one delicious hot dish.

While the soup's heating, you make the sandwiches. For each sandwich, put butter and peanut butter on one slice of bread; put honey on the second slice and then, "sandwich" together. The crunchy potato sticks simply spill out of the can into a serving dish. For the dessert, you reach into the cooky jar which is never empty—not the way you like to make and munch crisp cookies. Put the apples in a bowl, the cookies on a plate—to save yourself a trip back to the kitchen. Serve everyone a big glass of chilled milk.

**Family supper
—by you**

Egg-in-a-bun Sandwiches (*page 28*)
Sunny Carrots (*page 70*)
Baked Apples (*page 42*)   Cream
Sugar Drops (*page 32*)
Milk

You may want an assistant cook when it comes to getting a whole meal. If you want to do it alone, you can save time by filling the cooky jar the day before and baking the apples ahead of time. Let them wait in the refrigerator. If this is more than you want to tackle, do a switcheroo: Serve ice cream with the cookies, instead of the apples. The rest of the meal you can get ready in about a half hour before you plan to call supper. Clean the carrots and cut into strips before you get too busy. The egg baskets are hamburger buns. Cut a circle out of each bun, drop an egg in each, and bake. Then put a slice of cheese over bun and let it melt in oven.

**Picnic in the
back yard**

Frankfurters (*page 50*)
Catsup and Mustard
Potato Salad (*page 72*)   Sliced Tomatoes
Crisp Pickles
Ice-cream Pops (*page 40*)
Circustime Lemonade (*page 16*)

Everyone likes this kind of food on a picnic—piping-hot franks, potato salad, ice cream—you just can't miss. But, of course, you want to show a little genius, and that's where the Ice-cream Pops come in. You make them in the morning and let them freeze hard in the freezer. Each one has its own wooden-spoon handle for easy eating—even outdoors. If you wish, you can letter a name on each handle.

A picnic isn't supposed to be a lot of trouble, so take all the short cuts you can. Use frozen lemonade and skip the lemon squeezing. You won't even have to figure out how much sugar to use.

Count on paper plates, cups, napkins for your outdoor feast. They come in all colors and patterns. Save dishwashing!

**What to cook
for a crowd**

Saucy Spaghetti and Vienna Sausages (*page 56*)
Tossed Green Salad (*page 74*)
Brown-and-serve French Bread, Butter
Orange and Banana Ambrosia
Milk

Serve this buffet-style. Guests will pick up plates, napkins, and silverware. Then, they'll help themselves to the hot spaghetti, cool salad, crusty bread, butter, and milk. They can come back for dessert or you can pass it.

The spaghetti's all made for you. All it takes is a few turns of the can opener—and a few stirs of the spoon while it is heating. Be sure to double or triple the recipe if you have enough people to your party to make the extra food necessary.

To make the Ambrosia, peel and slice 1 banana and 2 oranges into a bowl. Add ¼ cup moist shredded coconut. Chill. Put in dessert dishes just before serving time, and top with maraschino cherries. This is enough to serve four. Double if needed.

Index